Joe DiMaggio
Baseball Star

Joe DiMaggio
Baseball Star

by Trudie Engel

Scholastic Inc.
New York Toronto London Auckland Sydney

PHOTO CREDITS

Black-and-white interior photos:

Cover photo:

Back cover photo:

ISBN 0-590-46067-6

12 11 10 9 8 7 6 5 4 3 2 1   3 4 5 6 7 8/9

Printed in the U.S.A.   40

First Scholastic printing, March 1994

For Al, Jon, Peter, Steve, Ken

Contents

1. The Family   1

2. The Neighborhood   6

3. Joe Goes Pro   13

4. Yankee Rookie   22

5. Yankee Clipper   31

6. The Streak   41

7. When the Going
   Gets Tough   51

8. The Great DiMaggio   60

Joe DiMaggio
Baseball Star

Joe DiMaggio is a hero to many, even young cowboys.

Chapter 1
The Family

"Here it comes, Joe!" Joe's sister Frances threw her best pitch.

It was 1920 in San Francisco.

Six-year-old Joe DiMaggio swung the broken paddle he used for a bat.

Joe didn't have a bat, so he hit the ball with anything he could get his hands on.

Like the old paddle from his father's fishing boat.

Pow! The ball sailed over his sister's head. It rolled down the steep hill behind the DiMaggios' house.

Frances ran after the ball. She came back puffing. Joe was hitting her pitches all over the place.

Soon Joe's big brother Vince gave him a real bat, and Joe began to play in the neighborhood pick-up games with his older brothers.

It wasn't long before Joe was hitting the neighborhood pitchers' best pitches all over the place, too.

By the time he was ten years old, Joe was always the first one chosen in the pick-up games.

Many of the games were played in a large dirt lot near Joe's house, called the horse lot. The milk company kept the horses that pulled the milk wagons there.

The neighborhood kids threw stones at the horses to drive them away.

They also used stones for bases and home plate. They played with an old ball held together with tape.

When Joe slammed a home run, the tape flew off the ball and the horses scattered.

The DiMaggios were supposed to have a rule about being late for supper. If the children weren't home on time, they wouldn't get anything to eat.

But they all knew Mama wouldn't really let anyone go hungry. So if a pick-up game was in the seventh inning, none of the boys would quit and hurry home.

Rosalie DiMaggio wouldn't get too angry if the children came in a little late for supper.

But she did get upset if one of the boys came in with torn pants. Their clothes were handed down from the older to the younger brothers.

There were eleven DiMaggios. Papa

Guiseppe, Mama Rosalie, and nine children, four girls and five boys. Joe was the second youngest.

The DiMaggios lived in a four-room house. All the girls slept in one bedroom and all the boys in another.

The family was poor, but so were most of the people in their neighborhood in those days.

But they were never so poor that any of the children went hungry or couldn't go to school because they had no shoes.

All the boys had to help earn money for the family.

Joe and his brothers sold newspapers on a busy street corner in the downtown part of San Francisco.

On their way home, the boys passed stores with boxes of candy and Cracker Jack piled up high in the windows.

They especially wanted the Cracker Jack. The baseball cards they collected were inside.

But Rosalie DiMaggio was very strict about money. The boys had to bring every penny they made home. She would sometimes give them a small allowance. It took Joe a long time to get a good collection of baseball cards.

Joe looked at his baseball cards every day. He studied the way the players held their bats. He looked hard at the players' faces.

He never dreamed that one day his own face would look back at him from a baseball card.

Chapter 2
The Neighborhood

The DiMaggios' house was halfway up the hill.

From its windows you could see the islands in San Francisco Bay. On clear days, the islands sparkled in the sunshine.

Before dawn every morning except Sunday, Guiseppe DiMaggio walked down the hill to the waterfront where he kept his fishing boat.

Hardly anyone in their neighborhood had a car. Schools, churches, stores, and playgrounds were nearby.

If people had to go someplace, they walked. If it was too far to walk, they took the streetcar.

People used streetcars to get around downtown San Francisco in the 1920s.

Rosalie DiMaggio and the children carried the groceries home from a little store on the corner.

Joe's school was only half a block away.

Like the DiMaggios, most of the other families in the neighborhood were Italian American.

Many of the men were fishermen. The women worked hard taking care of their families.

Joe's parents spoke Italian at home. They did not have time to learn to read or write English.

Later, Guiseppe DiMaggio did learn how to read a box score in the newspaper.

But when Joe was a kid, Guiseppe had no use for baseball. He wanted his sons to work with him on the family fishing boat.

Joe didn't like fishing. The tossing of the boat on the choppy waters made him sick. The smell of the fish made him sick, too.

Later, Joe said he wouldn't go near the fishing boat unless his family dragged him.

Joe spent all his extra time playing baseball. His older brothers, Tom and Vince, were also good ballplayers. They played in a semi-pro league.

Joe played for a Boys' Club team and became a better and better ballplayer. He could hit the ball harder and farther than anyone in the neighborhood.

A businessman who lived near the DiMaggios decided to sponsor a new semi-pro team. He had heard about Joe and asked him to be on the team. Joe couldn't wait to start.

For the first time, Joe played in a real uniform. He had a new glove and spikes.

Joe was the star of the team.

In a play-off game for the league championship, Joe hit two home runs. He hit the balls so far, they were never found.

His team won the game and the championship.

At a league awards ceremony, Joe was given two gold-plated baseballs and a gift certificate worth fifteen dollars.

Fifteen dollars was a lot of money in those days.

Being part of a large, close family and a friendly neighborhood was a big help to Joe in getting started in baseball.

Having older brothers in the game helped a lot. There were always neighborhood teams for him to play on.

But in some ways, the family and neighborhood were not so good for Joe.

Joe was very shy. With so many

brothers and sisters, he didn't have to make friends outside the family.

When he was little, if his brothers weren't on the playground, he'd hang around by himself and wouldn't talk to anyone.

Joe did all right in elementary and junior high school. But when he went to high school outside the neighborhood, he had a hard time.

Joe felt strange. He disliked meeting new people.

On the first day, many of the boys wore brand-new shirts and jackets to school. Joe was still in the old hand-me-downs he had worn in junior high.

He was scared of girls. When his sisters' girlfriends used to visit, he'd run out of the house so he wouldn't have to talk to them.

What he hated most about high school was having to answer the teachers' questions in class.

When Joe was fifteen, he quit high school. Since he wasn't going to school, he had to go to work to help the family.

Times were bad, and he had no skills. The only job Joe could find was in an orange juice factory.

He peeled oranges for eight hours a day.

It was, he said later, a really lousy way to make a living.

Chapter 3
Joe Goes Pro

Joe did not stay in the orange juice factory for long. As he peeled oranges, he asked himself: What do I like to do? What am I good at?

The answer, of course, was baseball.

Joe thought he could make a living playing ball. He was playing in a top semi-pro league.

His batting average was an amazing .633. Scouts from professional teams were looking at him.

Joe's brother Vince had signed a contract with the San Francisco Seals.

The Seals were the biggest team around. At that time, there were no major league teams in California.

Another minor league team offered Joe $150 a month to play for them.

Guiseppe DiMaggio couldn't get over it. One hundred fifty dollars a month for throwing some balls around! That was more than *he* made working 70 hours a week on his fishing boat.

Before making up his mind, Joe wanted to talk things over with Vince.

Vince was at Seal Stadium. The Seals were in the middle of a ball game.

Joe didn't have enough money to buy a ticket to get in. He was too proud to ask for a free pass.

So he stood outside the stadium looking in through a hole in the fence.

A scout from the Seals who had seen Joe play came along. "Aren't you Vince's kid brother?" he asked.

Joe nodded shyly.

The scout led Joe inside the stadium. Instead of taking Joe to a seat in the bleachers, the scout took him to the owner's office.

He told the owner all about Joe.

The Seals were at the end of a bad season. The owner thought a hitter like Joe could help the Seals.

Joe forgot all about the other team.

He played in three games with the Seals in 1932. His first time at bat, he hit a triple.

The Seals asked him to report to training camp next spring. Before long, he had a contract for $225 a month.

That was twice as much as most rookies made.

When the season opened, Joe was sitting on the bench.

The Seals had him playing shortstop.

He had a great throwing arm, but shortstop was not a good position for Joe.

In one game, the Seals were losing 6–1 and needed runs badly. The manager sent Joe in as a pinch hitter for the right fielder.

Joe walked. But the next day, he started in right field and got two hits.

Joe had found his position. From then on, he played in the outfield. He was on his way to the top.

As an outfielder, Joe quickly became the Seals' biggest star.

Here is his record for his rookie year in professional baseball:

Games Played	187
Batting Average	.340
Home Runs	28
Runs Batted In	169

oe DiMaggio (right) and two teammates from the San
rancisco Seals in 1935.

Most amazing of all, Joe broke the league record for a hitting streak. He hit safely in 61 games in a row. The old record was 49 games.

Joe was only 18 years old. He was the hottest player in the minors. All the major league teams had their eyes on him.

Then Joe hurt his knee badly. For a while, his leg was in a metal splint. He missed many games during his second season.

Some of the major league teams lost interest. But Joe's favorite team, the New York Yankees did not.

The Yankees' great hitter, Babe Ruth, was getting old. The team needed a new, young slugger in the line-up. They thought they had found one in Joe DiMaggio.

Before going to the Yankees, Joe played one more year with the Seals.

His last season with the Seals was outstanding. He batted .398 and hit 34 home runs. He led the league in RBIs.

And he learned something that would be very important when he played for the Yankees.

The Seals' new manager showed him how to hit the ball so it would go far into left field. Yankee Stadium had the deepest left field of all the major league ballparks.

A right-handed hitter like Joe had to pull the ball sharply to hit a home run in Yankee Stadium.

On a cold gray morning in February 1936, a shiny new Ford sedan pulled up in front of the DiMaggios' house.

Inside the car were two Yankee players. They were going to drive Joe to Florida for spring training.

Nineteen-year-old Joe was still very shy. He had never been away from home for long. He had never lived outside his own neighborhood.

Joe said good-bye to his parents and got into the backseat of the car.

For most of the way to Florida, Joe sat without saying a word. He looked out the window watching America roll by.

The other two Yankee players took turns driving. At last one said, "Don't you think we should let the kid drive?"

"Yeah," said the other player. He turned to Joe in the backseat.

"Want to drive, kid?" he asked.

Joe didn't answer for a long time.

Then he said, "I don't know how."

oe says good-bye to his family as he leaves for the Yankees'
raining camp in 1936.

Chapter 4
Yankee Rookie

"So you're the great DiMaggio," a tough Yankee pitcher said to Joe at spring training camp.

Joe knew that rookies got teased. He also knew how a rookie was supposed to act.

Joe just shrugged his shoulders and walked away.

When people kidded him, Joe kept his mouth shut. He let his bat talk for him.

At spring practice, he got so many good hits that the sports writers called him "the new Babe Ruth."

During a practice game, Joe hurt his foot sliding into second base. The trainer put Joe's foot into a special heat-ray machine to help it get better.

But something was wrong with the machine and it got much too hot.

Joe didn't know it was not working properly. He was too shy to tell anyone that the machine was burning him.

By the time the trainer got back, Joe's foot was badly burned.

He had to sit on the bench during the season opener.

The Yankees played 16 games without Joe. Joe waited and waited for his foot to heal.

One cold day in May, Joe walked from his hotel to Yankee Stadium. He was neatly dressed in a white shirt, dark suit, and tie.

All the Yankee players had to dress up

when they were out in public. No Yankee was ever seen checking into a hotel in a T-shirt.

That day, the manager watched Joe closely during batting practice. He seemed to be moving all right.

"You're in, DiMaggio," he told Joe.

It looked like it was about to rain. Only 11,000 fans had braved the chilly winds to come out to the ball game.

Joe batted third. He faced a big, right-handed pitcher. The first pitch whizzed by Joe. Then he lined the second pitch into left field for a single.

When the first game was over, Joe had three hits in six times at bat. He was batting .500.

Joe went on to a wonderful rookie season.

He finished his first year (1936) with

the Yankees with a .323 batting average, 29 home runs, and 125 RBIs. And he led the league in outfield assists.

Many years later, the Yankee manager said, "Joe was the best rookie I ever saw break in."

Joe turned out to be as good in the field as he was at bat. Joe was the Yankee's center fielder.

Yankee Stadium had a huge outfield. Joe had to cover a lot of territory.

Joe hardly ever missed a fly ball. He seemed to know just where the ball was going.

Knowing what the ball was going to do also made Joe an excellent base runner. He could tell when to stretch a single into a double or when he could make it to third on a base hit.

Just once the ball didn't do what Joe

Joe had a great rookie season in 1936 playing for the
New York Yankees.

expected. He hit a line drive into center field. He sped around the bases and was thrown out at third.

"What happened, Joe?" The manager asked.

"I saw the ball way out there and thought I could make it to third," Joe said. "Only when I looked again, I saw it wasn't the ball. It was a bird."

That was one of the few times Joe made a mistake running the bases.

With Joe DiMaggio's help, the Yankees went on to win the American League championship. They played the New York Giants in the World Series.

Joe brought his brother Tom and his mother, Rosalie, out from San Francisco to watch the World Series. They rode four and a half days on the train to get to New York.

Joe's mother was very proud of her son the baseball star.

Rosalie DiMaggio still spoke almost no English. One newspaper sent a reporter who spoke Italian to talk to her.

In Italian Mrs. DiMaggio told the

reporter, "My son, Joe, will win."

The sixth game of the World Series was played at Yankee Stadium.

The President of the United States, Franklin D. Roosevelt, was at the game.

In the last half of the ninth inning, the Giants were at bat. There were two outs. The Yankees needed one more victory to win the series.

A Giant player hit the ball far into center field. It headed toward the fence.

Joe always played center field close in behind second base. Rosalie DiMaggio watched as her son raced back after the ball.

Joe leaped up and caught the ball right in front of the fence. The ball had traveled 460 feet into Joe's glove.

Joe's great catch won the game. The Yankees beat the Giants in the World

Series, 4 games to 2.

The players were told to stay on the field while President Roosevelt was driven out through the center-field gate.

Joe DiMaggio stood alone in deep center field. As the President drove by in an open car, he gave Joe the thumbs-up sign.

It was a moment Joe never forgot. It was also a moment Rosalie DiMaggio never forgot.

With his share of the World Series prize money, Joe bought a big stone house in a beautiful part of San Francisco for his parents.

Chapter 5
Yankee Clipper

The 1937 season was even better for Joe. He won the American League home run championship with 46 home runs. He raised his batting average to .346.

The Yankees won the league championship again. They went on to beat the Giants in the World Series, 4 games to 1.

Joe became one of the most famous ballplayers in America.

Sports writers wrote many stories about him. He got more than 20 letters a day from fans.

He went to Hollywood to be in a movie. There he met a beautiful young actress named Dorothy Arnold.

Joe said only one line in the movie. He said a little more to Dorothy. They began to date.

Joe's third year in the major leagues got off to a bad start.

Professional ballplayers have many reasons for playing the game.

Some do it for fun. Some because they want to be the best. For others, it's the money that's important.

Joe loved baseball and always tried hard to do his very best.

But money mattered to Joe, too.

His family had been poor. Eleven DiMaggios had lived in a four-room house.

Joe wanted to help his family. Besides the new house, Joe bought a new fishing boat for his brother Mike.

He put a lot of his money into another family business. The brothers opened a restaurant on Fisherman's Wharf in San Francisco called DiMaggio's Grotto.

Joe worried about getting hurt and not being able to make money playing ball. He had already been hurt badly two times.

Joe knew he was a very, very good ballplayer. He asked the Yankees for more money.

They said they would pay him $25,000. Joe turned it down. He wanted $40,000.

Yankee spring training began without Joe DiMaggio. He stayed in San Francisco, a holdout.

The Yankee owners said he would not get a penny more than $25,000.

Joe heard many stories. He heard the

Yum! Joe tasting spaghetti at the DiMaggio's restaurant in San Francisco.

Yankees were planning to sell him to another team.

He heard that a new center fielder was coming to take his place.

In the end, he had to give in. He signed a contract for $25,000.

The fans weren't happy with Joe. They thought he had asked for too much. Joe was booed the first time he came to bat.

Joe DiMaggio wasn't used to that! Maybe it was the booing that threw him off. During the first game, Joe and the second baseman both went after the same fly ball.

They bumped into each other going full speed.

Joe and the second baseman were knocked out cold and had to be carried off the field on stretchers.

SAFE! Joe's run tied the score in the ninth inning. The Yankees had three more runs in an extra inning and won the 1939 World Series.

But the next day, Joe was back and hit a home run.

The following year, 1939, was a great one for Joe. He batted .381.

He was well on the way to breaking .400 when an eye infection made it hard for him to hit.

In 1939, Joe was named the Most Valuable Player in the American League.

The Yankees won the American League pennant again. In the World Series, they beat the Cincinnati Reds 4 games to 2.

It was also in 1939 that Joe married Dorothy Arnold.

He was married in Saints Peter and Paul's Cathedral in San Francisco. It was the church he had attended while growing up.

It seemed as if the whole Italian-American neighborhood and half of the rest of the city turned out for Joe's wedding.

More than 10,000 people crowded into the square in front of the church.

The police had to clear the way for the bride and groom.

Joe's brother Vince was the best man. The streets were so crowded that Vince was a half hour late for the wedding.

By the time he got to the church, the front door was locked, and he couldn't get in.

Vince finally got in by a side door. When he opened the door, twelve uninvited people slipped in with him.

After the wedding, there was a big party at DiMaggio's Grotto.

The mayor of San Francisco was there. So were Guiseppe DiMaggio's fishermen friends.

A band played Italian music. The guests ate twelve turkeys, eight hams, fifteen chickens, and four sides of beef!

The next year, Joe led the league in hitting again. But it was 1941 that turned out to be Joe's most exciting season in baseball.

It's going…it's going…it's gone!

Chapter 6
The Streak

On May 15, 1941, the Yankees were playing the Chicago White Sox.

It was a cool, cloudy afternoon at Yankee Stadium.

Joe DiMaggio came up to bat. He slammed a single to left-center field. He only hit one out of four that day, but in the next game, he hit safely again.

And in the game after that. And in the game after that one, too.

In every game in May, Joe got at least one hit.

After he had hit in 20 games in a row, people started to talk about a streak.

Fans crowded into the ballparks to see Joe play.

Even when people started talking about a batting streak, Joe was steady as ever.

The best pitchers in the league were put up against him. They tried to make him swing at bad pitches.

But Joe stayed cool.

He didn't care who was pitching or

what kind of pitches were thrown.

He never changed his batting style. He stood up straight at the plate. He kept his legs about two feet apart.

Joe held his head level, with his eyes fixed on the ball as it came toward him. He held his bat still until he swung.

Joe hardly ever struck out. He was probably the steadiest ballplayer ever.

It seemed as if he could hit the ball whenever he wanted.

All during June, Joe kept hitting in game after game.

On June 17, he passed the 30-game mark.

On June 28, he hit in his 40th game.

The old record was 41 games. It had been set back in 1922.

The next game would decide if Joe could tie the record for a hitting streak.

A hit in the game after that would break it.

Games number 41 and 42 were played as a doubleheader in Washington, DC. It was June 29, a boiling hot day with the temperature going up to 100 degrees in the afternoon.

In the sixth inning of the first game, Joe hit a double deep into left center field.

The fans went wild. Joe had tied the record.

Now, would he go on to break it?

Between games, Joe rested in the clubhouse. He drank a cup of coffee and changed his shirt.

When he came out, he headed for the bat rack.

His bat was gone! Someone had stolen it after the first game.

Like most ballplayers, Joe had a favorite bat. It was a Louisville Slugger, model 2–29.

Joe had rubbed his bat with olive oil to make it smooth. He had sanded it so he could get a good grip.

All of Joe's streak hits had been made with that bat. The Yankees hunted wildly for the bat. It could not be found.

It was Joe's turn to bat.

Tommy Henrich, the Yankee's right fielder, also used the model 2–29. He told Joe to use his.

But Joe didn't like the idea of playing with someone else's bat. He grabbed one of his back-up bats and went to the plate.

Joe hit a wobbly ball to right field. The fielder scooped it up. Joe was out at first.

His second time at bat, he lined out to the shortstop.

In the fifth inning, he hit a pop fly to center field.

Joe was up once more in the seventh inning. This might be his last time at bat. It could be his last chance to break the record.

"Joe," Tommy Henrich said again, "try my bat. It's got a real good feel."

Joe just stood there, looking at the pitcher.

"Okay," he said to Tommy at last. "Let me have your bat."

The first pitch was inside, a fastball. Joe had to lean way back to keep from getting hit.

The next one, he figured, would be slow and outside. Joe watched the ball as it floated in toward him.

Joe sets a new record in 1941 for hitting safely in 42 games!

He swung.

Crack! He drove a hard single into left field.

The roar of the crowd shook the stadium. The whole Yankee team jumped off the bench. They all cheered for Joe.

Joe never was a big talker. "Sure, I'm tickled," he said after the game.

George Sisler, the old-record holder, said, "I'm glad a real hitter broke it. Keep it up."

And that's just what Joe did. When he hit safely in the next game, the fans cheered for five minutes.

Joe kept on hitting in game after game.

On July 11, he had hit in 50 games.

Joe's streak was front-page news all over the country.

A summer high school class was asked to pick the three most famous Americans that ever lived.

On their list, Abraham Lincoln came in third. George Washington was second. And Joe DiMaggio was in first place.

Everywhere, radio stations were playing a song about Joe. It went like this:

He'll live in Baseball's Hall of Fame.

He got there blow by blow.

Our kids will tell their kids his name —

Joltin' Joe DiMaggio.

It was a night game in Cleveland on July 17, 1941.

The Indians' star third baseman somehow stopped two of Joe's hard grounders and whipped them to first.

Joe grounded out to the shortstop in his last time at bat.

The streak was over. It had lasted for 56 games. "In a way I'm glad," Joe told reporters.

During the streak he had seemed calm and sure of himself.

But later he said, "I was able to control myself. But that doesn't mean I wasn't dying inside."

It is now more than fifty years since Joe's hitting streak made baseball history.

In all that time, no one has come close to hitting in 56 games in a row.

Joe's record still stands. Many people say it will never be broken.

Chapter 7
When the
Going Gets Tough

It was 1945. World War II had been fought and won. The soldiers were coming home from the war.

Joe DiMaggio had spent three years in the Air Force. He had missed three seasons with the Yankees.

Now he was back. With his four-year-old son, also called Joe DiMaggio, he went to Yankee Stadium to see his team play.

Holding little Joe by the hand, he tried to slip into Yankee Stadium without being seen.

But the fans spotted him.

As father and son went to their seats, a great cheer filled the stadium.

Joe and his son pose for a photograph.

"Joe, Joe, — Joe DiMaggio," the crowd chanted over and over.

Little Joe turned to his father. "Look Daddy," he said. "Everyone knows my name."

It was hard to come back in 1946. Joe was 32 years old. During Joe's first season after the war, it was not easy for him to get in shape. He had been hurt many times.

1947 was better. Joe won the Most Valuable Player award that year. And he led the Yankees to another American League championship.

The Yankees went on to beat the Brooklyn Dodgers in the World Series.

In the middle of the 1948 season, Joe's heel hurt badly. He also had trouble with a shoulder, a knee, and an elbow.

Home run! Joe scores in a game against the Red Sox.

From that time on, he never played ball without something hurting him.

In 1948, with all his aches and pains, Joe batted .320 and hit 39 home runs. He led the league with 155 RBIs.

The Yankees gave him a $100,000 contract for the next year.

During the off-season, Joe had an operation on his heel. Special spikes with a cushioned heel were made for him.

He tried to play in spring training, but his heel still hurt. Joe took himself out of the line-up and went back to the hospital for another operation.

In April, Joe looked out the hospital window and saw the trees had new green leaves. The baseball season had begun, and he could barely stand up.

Joe needed crutches to walk.

Then, one morning in late June, Joe got out of bed and found he could walk without pain in his heel.

He whistled for the first time in months.

That same day, Joe flew up to Boston where the Yankees were playing the Red Sox.

The two teams were in a tight race for first place in the American League. The winner would play in the World Series.

Joe rushed out to Fenway Park. It was a night game. The stands buzzed as Joe came up to bat.

"Can Joe still do it?" people asked each other. "Can he come back?"

Joe seemed as cool as ever. He stepped up to the plate and hit a single. The second time Joe was at bat he hit a home run.

The great star of the Red Sox was Ted Williams. He and Joe were the two best hitters in baseball.

In the ninth inning, Ted Williams hit a long ball to deep center field. Joe caught it to win the game.

The next day, Joe hit two home runs. The day after that, he hit another.

The Yankees won every game in their series against the Red Sox.

Joe was a team player. Nothing made him feel better than to see his team win.

Even if he had a great day himself, he would not be happy if the Yankees lost.

Now, after the Yankees had won four straight against the Red Sox with his help, he was all smiles.

"You can't beat this life, kid," he told

a Yankee rookie as he left the clubhouse that night.

But 1949 was not a happy year for Joe. His father died that year. His mother was very sick. And though they were still good friends, his marriage to Dorothy was over.

Later in the season, Joe caught pneumonia. He was in the hospital again.

With two games left to play, the Yankees and the Red Sox were tied for the league championship.

Joe came back to play in the last two games of the season. He was weak, and his legs were wobbly.

"It was a big lift for everybody, just having him out there," one of the players said.

The Yankees won the last two games and the World Series.

There is a saying, "When the going gets tough, the tough get going."

Joe showed the saying is true. He ended the season with a .346 batting average.

Chapter 8
The Great DiMaggio

"There he is!"

"That's him."

"Get his autograph."

Bits of paper were shoved at him. Joe signed as many as he could, then climbed into a taxi.

Joe DiMaggio was leaving Yankee Stadium. Wherever he went, it was the same.

Joe couldn't eat a meal in a restaurant without a crowd gathering.

But Joe always had time for the kids who hung around the stadium, hoping to get a close look or an autograph.

He was getting older and tiring faster. Still, he would play both ends of a

oe always had time to sign a few autographs for his fans.

doubleheader in case there was a kid in the stands who might not get to see him play.

The 1950 season was a tough one for Joe. Many nagging injuries kept him from playing his best. He couldn't run, throw, or hit the way he used to.

"I'm hitting flabby fly balls," he said.

The Yankees were in another tight pennant race. They had a new manager, Casey Stengel. They also had many good young players.

Stengel wanted to win. He did a number of things that Joe didn't like.

Stengel changed the line-up and tried players at different positions. He moved Joe down from fourth to fifth in the batting order.

Once he had Joe play first base instead of center field. He also benched

Joe and his teammate Mickey Mantle, the next great Yankee hitter.

Joe when he was in a batting slump.

In 1951, 19-year-old Mickey Mantle was the Yankee's big star. Joe was almost 37 years old. His batting average fell to .263.

Joe knew it was time to quit.

He played in one more World Series, against the Giants.

Three of the greatest center fielders of all time played in that 1951 series: Joe DiMaggio, Mickey Mantle, and Willie Mays.

At his last time at bat, Joe hit a hard line drive for a double.

When he pulled up at second base, the crowd cheered for a long time.

Did the people know it was Joe's last hit in major league baseball?

The Yankees would have paid Joe $100,000 for another year because he was so famous.

But Joe was too proud to play when he couldn't do his best.

In December 1952, Joe met with reporters at the Yankee office in New

York. First he read a speech that said he was leaving the game. Then he answered questions.

"Why are you quitting?" a reporter asked him.

"I don't have it anymore," Joe said simply.

Joe gave his built-up spikes and the bat he had rubbed with olive oil to his friend Billy Martin. Billy played second base for the Yankees. He was from the San Francisco area too.

Baseball's Hall of Fame is full of great players who have set world records.

But Joe DiMaggio was much more than just a good ballplayer.

Why do so many people think of him as a real hero?

People who have seen him play say

Joe at the ceremony in 1951 to honor him into the Hall of Fame.

that every move Joe made on the field looked good. And he made it all look easy.

He never hot dogged, or showed off to the crowd. He didn't make any diving catches. He caught fly balls with two hands.

Joe was a team leader. He didn't lose his temper, get into fights, or yell at the other players or at an umpire.

Joe's teammate, pitcher Allie Reynolds, said, "He gave a thousand percent in every game, day in, day out."

Ask the fans. Ask the "old guys" who can remember going out to Yankee Stadium back when they were eight or nine.

They'll tell you, "Joe DiMaggio really gave us something to cheer about."

The great Joe DiMaggio.

About the Author

Trudie Engel is a reading teacher in central Pennsylvania. She has four grown sons who are Pirate or Philly fans. Her husband, who saw Joe DiMaggio play many times, is still a Yankee fan.